INSTITUTE OF LEADERSHIP & MANAGEMENT

SUPERSERIES

Managing Tough Times

FOURTH EDITION

Published for the
Institute of Leadership & Management by **Pergamon** *Flexible* **Learning**

OXFORD AMSTERDAM BOSTON LONDON NEW YORK PARIS
SAN DIEGO SAN FRANCISCO SINGAPORE SYDNEY TOKYO

Pergamon Flexible Learning
An imprint of Elsevier Science
Linacre House, Jordan Hill, Oxford OX2 8DP
200 Wheeler Road, Burlington, MA 01803

First published 1986
Second edition 1991
Third edition 1997
Fourth edition 2003

Copyright © 1986, 1991, 1997, 2003, ILM
All rights reserved.

No part of this publication may be reproduced in any material form (including photocopying or storing in any medium by electronic means and whether or not transiently or incidentally to some other use of this publication) without the written permission of the copyright holder except in accordance with the provisions of the Copyright, Designs and Patents Act 1988 or under the terms of a licence issued by the Copyright Licensing Agency Ltd, 90 Tottenham Court Road, London, England W1T 4LP. Applications for the copyright holder's written permission to reproduce any part of this publication should be addressed to the publisher

British Library Cataloguing in Publication Data
A catalogue record for this book is available from the British Library

ISBN 0 7506 5817 7

For information on Pergamon Flexible Learning
visit our website at www.bh.com/pergamonfl

Institute of Leadership & Management
registered office
1 Giltspur Street
London
EC1A 9DD
Telephone 020 7294 3053
www.i-l-m.com
ILM is a subsidiary of the City & Guilds Group

The views expressed in this work are those of the authors and do not necessarily reflect those of the Institute of Leadership & Management or of the publisher

Authors: Paul Shanahan and Dela Jenkins
Editor: Eileen Cadman
Editorial management: Genesys, www.genesys-consultants.com
Composition by Genesis Typesetting, Rochester, Kent
Printed and bound in Great Britain by MPG Books, Bodmin

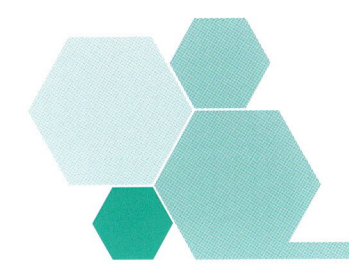

Contents

Workbook introduction v

1. ILM Super Series study links v
2. Links to ILM qualifications v
3. Links to S/NVQs in Management vi
4. Workbook objectives vi
5. Activity planner viii

Session A What makes your job tough? 1

1. Introduction 1
2. Types of working demand 1
3. Work-related demands 2
4. People demands 8
5. Demands from the changing world 11
6. Multiple demands 14
7. Summary 16

Session B How do you cope with tough times? 17

1. Introduction 17
2. What to look for 18
3. We are all different 21
4. The three stages of stress 22
5. How stress can affect your organization 26
6. Summary 32

Session C Helping yourself in tough times 33

1. Introduction 33
2. First aid 33
3. Preparing for tough times 41
4. Summary 47

Contents

Session D Helping others in tough times — 49

1. Introduction — 49
2. Promoting teamwork — 49
3. Supporting and advising, counselling and mentoring — 51
4. Summary — 59

Performance checks — 61

1. Quick quiz — 61
2. Workbook assessment — 64
3. Work-based assignment — 65

Reflect and review — 69

1. Reflect and review — 69
2. Action plan — 72
3. Extensions — 74
4. Answers to self-assessment questions — 75
5. Answers to the quick quiz — 78
6. Feedback on Activity 13 — 80
7. Certificate — 80

Workbook introduction

1 ILM Super Series study links

This workbook addresses the issues of *Managing Tough Times*. Should you wish to extend your study to other Super Series workbooks covering related or different subject areas, you will find a comprehensive list at the back of this book.

2 Links to ILM qualifications

This workbook relates to the following learning outcomes in segments from the ILM Level 3 Introductory Certificate in First Line Management and the Level 3 Certificate in First Line Management.

C1.4 Manage Own Stress
1 Understand stress and its potential causes
2 Recognize symptoms of stress in oneself
3 Understand the effects of stress on own work performance and on others
4 Identify means of reducing own stress
5 Develop a personal stress management plan to maintain a work/life balance

C7.7 Supporting Individuals
1 Understand the difference between counselling, advising and mentoring and when each is appropriate in the workplace

Workbook introduction

    C8.4   Minimizing Stress
1. Understand stress and its potential causes
2. Recognize the symptoms of stress in others
3. Understand the potential causes of stress
4. Appreciate the implications of stress for individuals and the organization
5. Take action to reduce the causes of stress within own area of responsibility
6. Identify support mechanisms for individuals already suffering from stress

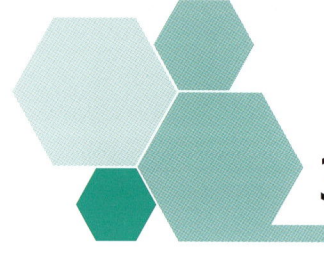

3 Links to S/NVQs in Management

This workbook relates to the following elements of the Management Standards which are used in S/NVQs in Management, as well as a range of other S/NVQs.

    A1.2   Maintain healthy, safe and productive working conditions
    C15.1   Help team members who have problems affecting their performance

It will also help you develop the following Personal Competences:

- building teams;
- focusing on results.

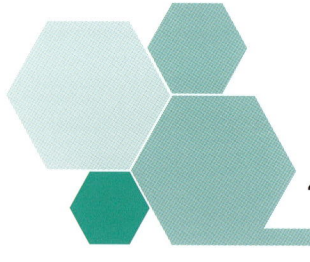

4 Workbook objectives

Working life can bring many good things: money, security, satisfaction, social contacts, a sense of identity. It also usually brings problems. A lot of the time these are routine, everyday problems that we just accept as a normal and predictable part of our jobs. But sometimes these problems can become so severe, so numerous or so long-lasting that all of the good things are put at

Workbook introduction

risk. These are the tough times that most of us experience at some point in our working careers.

Tough times can be on a large scale, affecting maybe millions of people, such as the recessions of the 1980s and early 1990s. Sometimes particular industries suffer their own tough times, such as the IT industry in 'Silicon Valley', California or the airline industry in recent years.

Tough times can also be on a much more personal scale. You have probably witnessed cases where an individual's marriage problems have spilled over into their working life. You may have had to break the news of impending redundancy to a long-standing employee whose job has disappeared in some organizational restructuring.

This workbook is designed to help you as a team leader manage tough times effectively. You will learn to recognize the early warning signs that times are getting tough. You will explore how you react yourself when the going gets tough. How you manage will be important in how the others around you react. You will learn to recognize when your team members and other colleagues and managers are having their own tough times. Often you will be the person best placed to help. As well as learning **when** to help, you will learn the basic principles of **how** to help. We will also look at how you can turn a tough time into something positive.

4.1 Objectives

When you have completed this workbook you will be better able to:

- recognize what makes your job tough;
- understand how you and other people typically react in tough times;
- take action to help yourself and others manage tough times;
- exploit the opportunities hidden in even the toughest of times.

Workbook introduction

5 Activity planner

The following Activities require some planning so you may want to look at these now.

- Activity 19 Which asks you to analyse a situation in which you were stressed.
- Activity 28 Which asks you to set up a stress reduction programme.
- Activity 36 Which asks you to analyse a situation where you helped a team member with a personal problem.

Some or all of these Activities may provide the basis of evidence for your S/NVQ portfolio. All Portfolio Activities and the Work-based assignment are signposted with this icon.

The icon states the elements to which the Portfolio Activities and Work-based assignment relate.

The Work-based assignment on page 65 suggests you discuss with at least two members of your team a tough time you all experienced. You might like to start thinking about whom you should approach, and perhaps arrange a time to have a chat with them. This assignment should be useful in helping to demonstrate your competence in:

- recognizing stress in yourself;
- being sensitive to the needs of others;
- helping team members who have problems affecting their performance.

Session A
What makes your job tough?

1 Introduction

Many supervisors and team leaders find their jobs demanding. Often it is in tackling and overcoming the problems that work throws at them, that they find enjoyment and satisfaction. Nobody who wants an easy life is likely to choose one of these difficult roles.

But many people in these positions are also finding that their jobs are getting a lot more difficult. As the demands increase, many supervisors and team leaders are experiencing feelings of stress, doubt, insecurity, uncertainty and anxiety. Many of the people around them at work are having similar uncomfortable feelings.

When these feelings of stress, fear and threat do not rapidly disappear, but persist over a lengthy period, then this is a 'tough time'. In a tough time there is a risk that the outer demands will overwhelm your inner resources. In this first session of the workbook we look at the demands which are likely to be placed on you in your work.

2 Types of working demand

What you feel as a **demand** rather than something you take in your stride is a very personal matter. Spend a few minutes thinking about what, if anything, makes your job hard going.

Session A

Activity 1 · *3 mins*

List five broad types of demand that make your job tough.

1. _____
2. _____
3. _____
4. _____
5. _____

You have probably listed a wide variety of things that make your job tough. Most of them can probably be grouped under one of the following headings:

- demands arising directly from the work you do;
- people problems;
- change.

We will now look at each of these kinds of demand in more detail.

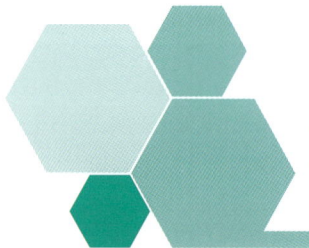

3 Work-related demands

'He does one damn thing after another' was the comment of one observer of a field sales manager's day. Brevity, variety and fragmentation seem to be par for the course for most managers.[1]

When times are especially tough you may feel as if everything is being piled up on top of you. But in reality you probably have to deal with demands of a number of different kinds. If you are going to respond successfully to these demands it is important that you can sort out the various demands you are facing from what may feel like a total mess.

[1] Handy, C. *Understanding Organizations*. 4th Edition, Penguin, 1999, pp. 320–1.

Session A

3.1 Time demands

Too much to do, too little time! A feature of many tough times is time pressure.

Activity 2 · 3 mins

Have you experienced time pressures becoming more severe in recent times? If so, what do you think has caused this?

_____

_____

A number of features of modern working life add to time pressures. As business has become more competitive, many companies have reorganized their ways of working, striving to remove 'slack' and become more efficient. Methods such as Just In Time (JIT) have been introduced to avoid having to maintain high levels of expensive stock, deliveries of new stock arriving just as they are needed. Staffing levels are cut to the absolute minimum.

3.2 Mental demands

All jobs make mental demands; some more than others. Observing and thinking take time, trouble and energy.

Activity 3 · 3 mins

First line managers have to think about many things. List below the main things that you usually have to keep in your mind as you go about your job.

_____

_____

_____

_____

Session A

A lot of your mental energy is of course spent on thinking about the work for which you are responsible. You will be concerned with how current work is progressing and what problems most urgently need your attention. You will also probably spend a lot of time planning how the work is going to proceed into the future.

As well as people, you may be in charge of materials, equipment, vehicles, budgets, workspace, and so on. This means that you have to keep many things in your head at the same time. The more you have to think about, and the more rapidly circumstances are changing, then the heavier the mental demands placed on you.

A demand on your mental energy that is likely to have become increasingly heavy in recent years is **information**. Many supervisors and team leaders complain of 'information overload'. This happens when you are bombarded with a mass of information which you must sift through – often under time pressure – to find out what needs your attention and what you can safely ignore.

Activity 4

3 mins

Do you suffer from information overload? If so, what is the main cause of this?

_____

_____

Many first line managers complain that they never get to the bottom of their in-trays – or nowadays to the end of their queue of e-mail messages. Computers have been one obvious cause of information overload, although in some businesses the culprit is the photocopier. But while it is easy to blame the technology, what is more important is the way it is used. Technology has indeed made it much easier to send out masses of information to many people, but this means that everyone must be far more careful in choosing what to send out, who to send it to, and how it is presented. For example, who really needs to receive minutes of that meeting? Does it really need four pages? Would not a half-page summary of decisions and actions be enough? Is it really necessary to copy e-mails to all and sundry so frequently?

Session A

3.3 Emotional demands

To be successful in your job you must be committed to what you and your team achieve; you must care about results and also how you work. Many of the emotional demands that arise from your work are to do with your customers, your staff, your managers, your colleagues and so on. We shall look at these human demands more closely later. But you may do work that is emotionally demanding in itself. Staff working in health care are, on occasions, likely to find it emotionally demanding dealing with patients in pain or relatives in distress. Staff in the emergency or social services face similar emotional demands in dealing with the victims of natural disaster, accidents or crime.

Emotional demands also arise where there is:

- financial risk;
- physical danger;
- intense competition;
- difficult decisions.

Activity 5 (5 mins)

Gupta is a supervisor in a medium sized insurance broker's office. He has been tasked with buying five new personal computers for his department. Although he has used computers for years, he has very limited technical knowledge. He has collected a mass of information from magazines and computer suppliers. This has given him lots of technical facts but does not tell him about the reliability of each model and the chances that the supplier will be around long enough to provide the after-sales support Gupta knows they will need. He is tempted to go for one of the well-known manufacturers as he has been told that their PCs are reliable, but he knows that they are very expensive. Gupta has to decide soon, as he been told to place an order within the next week, before the end of his company's financial year.

What makes Gupta's decision so difficult? How do you think Gupta feels about making this decision?

_____

_____

_____

_____

Session A

Difficult decisions such as Gupta's usually involve a high degree of uncertainty. On the one hand, he is feeling overwhelmed and out of his depth in trying to make sense of all the technical facts he has gathered. On the other hand, he does not have the information which tells him what he most needs to know. For many decisions you do not have all the information you need. You do not know what all the options are, and for those you do know about you do not know completely what the costs or benefits may be. Gupta is tempted to go for a well-known brand, but fears that he will be criticized for paying too much. If he goes for one of the cheaper, less well-known models, he may find that the computers are unreliable or the supplier fails to provide maintenance. Again, he fears he will get the blame. Gupta knows he could make a reasonable decision if he had time to get proper advice, but the time pressure rules this out. To sum up, Gupta probably feels helpless and hopeless, and also resentful.

Activity 6 · 2 mins

Can you think of a situation where having to deal with too many unknowns was emotionally draining for you?

_____

_____

_____

3.4 Physical demands

It is often easy to overlook the most obvious of work demands – the physical ones. We take for granted our working conditions and practices, and yet these can have a strong impact on our health and wellbeing. Here are some examples of physical demands:

- workplace too hot, cold, noisy;
- use of computer screens in poor lighting;
- badly designed chairs and desks;
- need to walk up and down stairs many times;
- driving a lot.

Session A

3.5 Peaks, troughs and the unexpected

In practice your job is probably not equally demanding all the time. Some times will be worse than others.

> Jim works in a signalling centre controlling a stretch of railway line in south west London. Jim and his assistant control a suburban station, a busy junction, and a series of level crossings. In the morning and evening rush hours, traffic on the railway and on roads using the crossings is heavy. The signalmen are then working flat out. In the middle of the day and in the later evening there is not a lot to do, and the bigger problem is boredom. Problems can arise from a variety of incidents, such as failure of a CCTV camera used to monitor the crossings. Surprisingly frequently, vehicles crash into the crossings trying to 'beat the barriers'. On occasions the traffic on their lines is increased by trains diverted from other lines to allow for engineering works. In the quieter times Jim and his assistant can usually comfortably deal with these additions to their workload. If they occur during rush hours, however, then the signalbox team can find themselves struggling to cope.

Activity 7

5 mins

Do you have predictable fluctuations in your workload? What kinds of non-routine demands can arise in your work? What effect do these additional demands have on your work and the work of your team?

_____

_____

_____

_____

In most kinds of work there are peaks and troughs. These may be daily, weekly, monthly, seasonal, annual, or times of economic boom and bust.

In addition to predictable peaks and troughs, you may find you have a great variety of unexpected demands. A customer may suddenly demand a rush job. An advertising campaign may be unexpectedly successful, leading to a sudden

Session A

increase in orders. A machine may break down or a member of your team may be absent without warning. These kinds of incidents add to your workload, but more seriously they tend to disrupt normal working patterns, adding to your existing time, mental and emotional demands. This increases the risk of mistakes being made. More mistakes will add still further to your workload, creating a vicious circle.

4 People demands

We have given the demands connected with people special treatment, as for many supervisors and team leaders these demands are often the main causes of tough times. Let us look at the main groups of people who can affect how tough your working life is.

4.1 Your team

As a first line manager, the people who will affect you most directly are the people you supervise or lead. Much of the pleasure or pain of your working life will be the result of how your team members behave.

Activity 8 · 3 mins

Which of the following problems have you experienced in the last six months with members of your team?

- poor timekeeping;
- absenteeism;
- persistent sickness;
- disciplinary problems;
- bad performance at work;
- personal problems affecting behaviour at work (e.g. sick child, divorce, drink, drugs, problems with the law);
- interpersonal conflicts;
- dishonesty or theft;
- compulsory redundancy;
- other (please specify) _____.

You have been fortunate if you have not suffered from some or all of these people problems. While these are causes of your own tough times, it is important to remember that they can probably be traced back to a tough time that the team member was having him or herself. We look more fully at what you can reasonably do to help, and how you should do it, in Session D.

4.2 Your manager

EXTENSION 1
If a difficult boss is a source of your tough times, you may want to look at Robert Bramson's book *Coping with Difficult Bosses*.

Managers can often seem to be a source of unreasonable demands. Here it is important to be as objective as possible. You need to accept that your manager may actually have legitimate reasons for turning down some request you have made, or for asking you to take on some difficult task. Hopefully your manager will explain these reasons to you, but, even if this does not happen, you still need to remain open to the possibility that these demands are indeed fair and reasonable.

On the other hand, it is undoubtedly true that managers are not always reasonable or helpful.

4.3 Your customers

Customers can also make your life difficult. They can make unreasonable demands, be offensive, complain, keep changing their minds, be vague, or be dishonest. In other words, customers can be difficult in similar ways to managers and team members.

4.4 Your family and friends

There can often be a tension between our working lives and our family and social lives. The people who are important to us outside work can also place demands on us that may cause or add to our tough times.

Session A

Activity 9
5 mins

Which of the following demands have you experienced from your life outside work?

- partners who complain about the time you spend at work;
- partners who complain about your level of income;
- babies or young children who keep you awake at night;
- family or social commitments that conflict with your work commitments;
- expectations from family or friends about the kind of work you do;
- expectations from family or friends about you getting promoted;
- other (please specify) _____.

How have these demands affected you at work?

_____
_____
_____
_____
_____

Parents, partners, children, even friends, may all place demands on you that affect your capacities at work. Some of these demands may be legitimate, some may be unreasonable, and some may just be facts of life (babies **do** wake at night, for example). At their simplest these demands can make you too tired to work at your best, or can require you to take time off work. More subtly, demands and expectations from family and friends can make you dissatisfied or frustrated in your job. These are feelings that can also reduce your level of performance. As you do less well, your dissatisfaction and frustration increase and you are on the way towards tough times.

4.5 Yourself

It is also worth asking to what extent **you** are a source of unreasonable demands on yourself.

Session A

Activity 10
10 mins

Note down any ways in which you think you may be contributing to your own tough times.

_____
_____
_____

Are you highly ambitious? Are you a perfectionist? Are you highly self-critical if you make a mistake? Do you have fears about your job security that are out of proportion to the risks? Are you over-concerned about being popular with your team? Are you too willing to take on extra responsibilities at work? Do you have trouble saying 'no'? Do you take on too many commitments outside of work? If you think your answers to these questions and others like them are 'yes', then you may be your own worst enemy.

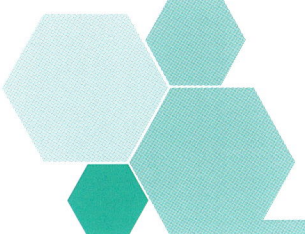

5 Demands from the changing world

For many people the world of work over the last few years has seemed to become a less certain, less safe, less comfortable place to be. Everything seems to be changing, and the speed of change seems to be getting faster. The consequences of these changes and how you can manage the process of change are dealt with in *Managing Change* in this series and are not repeated here. In this workbook we want to concentrate on how these changes can be the causes of tough times.

5.1 Threats to job security

> ... There are growing numbers of people who are insecure, fearful for their jobs in an age of permanent 'down-sizing', 'cost-cutting' and 'casualisation' and ever more worried about their ability to maintain a decent standard of living.'[1]

[1] Hutton, W. *The State We're In*. Revised Edition. Vintage, 1996.

Session A

High levels of unemployment have become a permanent feature of the British economy and indeed of economies across Europe. This is a tragedy for those without jobs and also a real cause of worry for those in work. The question is whether you consider this kind of threat as 'an act of God', over which you have no control, or whether you take positive action to prepare yourself for such a possibility. We look at how you can do this in Session C.

You may also find yourself having to deal with redundancy affecting members of your own team. This is likely to be stressful for them and you. We look specifically at this in Session D.

5.2 The changing role of the first line manager

In the 1990s many businesses have restructured or 're-engineered' in pursuit of more cost-effective ways of working. Often part of these changes has been 'de-layering': the removal of one or more levels of management hierarchy. There has also been a move towards greater reliance on multiskilled teams with a high degree of autonomy. On the one hand, these changes have opened up new opportunities to many first line managers. They have more responsibility and more chance to make real decisions for themselves. On the other hand, many first line managers, although willing to take on these more demanding roles, feel ill-equipped for their new jobs.

Activity 11 · 5 mins

Has your job changed in the last year or two? Did you feel sufficiently well-prepared to take on extra or different responsibilities? Was your team properly prepared?

_____
_____
_____

In my experience many supervisors have been asked to take on new responsibilities before they or their teams were really trained and prepared to do so. A particular difficulty is that often in the new organizations many of the old certainties about who did what have gone. The resulting uncertainty can be extremely uncomfortable and even stressful.

Session A

5.3 Obsolete knowledge and skills

A problem for many people at work these days is keeping their knowledge and skills up-to-date.

Activity 12
5 mins

What new skills and knowledge have you had to acquire in the last five years? How easy was it for you to do this?

_____

_____

_____

Technology is the area of rapid change that has most obviously needed new skills. Many people have, for example, had to master the basic use of a PC or Mac. But many other areas besides technology have also developed rapidly. Laws and regulations (e.g. company law, health and safety regulations) have changed. The very ways in which businesses operate have also changed as a result of privatization (e.g. telecommunications, electricity, rail) or deregulation (e.g. the financial and banking sectors).

All these changes lead to people fearing that their knowledge and skills will rapidly become obsolete, reducing their chances of getting or keeping a good job. They also have to spend time, effort, and maybe money, acquiring new skills and knowledge. This adds to the demands of one's current work. For many older people there is a special fear that they can no longer retain new knowledge or learn new skills in the way they did when they were younger.

5.4 Changing attitudes

Many social attitudes have changed in recent years. Of special significance here is changed attitudes towards authority. Many staff are reluctant to accept whatever they are told just because it comes from a person in authority. This may be a positive development, but for supervisors – who can no longer

Session A

simply hide behind their 'badge' – it requires them to develop the self-confidence and competence to deal with questioning members of their teams.

5.5 Change fatigue

Given that change is happening rapidly around us all the time, many people find it harder to respond positively and creatively to the challenges it poses. In some organizations (in the public sector, for example) constant change has left some people feeling quite cynical and demoralized. When people experience change as being instituted for its own sake, they are unlikely to put their energies into making the change work. They will just shrug it off as another management gimmick, and wonder when the current round of change will be replaced by another one.

6 Multiple demands

Although in this session we have tried to separate out the various kinds of demand you are likely to face, in practice a really tough time is likely to involve many of these kinds of demand piled up on top of each other. Knowing where to begin to identify, sort out and prioritize all these problems is difficult but essential. Before you can start to take action on the problems themselves, you need to bring under control your own reactions to these problems. We turn to this in Session B.

Session A

Self-assessment 1

For questions 1 to 6 complete the sentences with a suitable word or words chosen from the following list:

| TROUGHS | PHYSICAL | MENTAL | PEAKS |
| OUTER | TIME | EMOTIONAL | INNER |

1 A time feels tough when the _____ demands exceed your _____ resources.

2 When all the 'slack' has been removed from your working methods you are likely to suffer from _____ pressure.

3 The more tasks, people and information you have to think about, the heavier are the _____ demands of your job.

4 If you are really committed to your work, you cannot avoid some _____ demands.

5 Poor furniture, bad lighting, stuffy air, and too much driving all add to the _____ demands of your work.

6 The demands you experience in your work will change according to the _____ and _____ in your workload.

7 Give three examples of groups of people that can create demands for you in your work.

_____ _____ _____

8 Give three examples of major changes that have tended to make working life more tough these days than in earlier times.

_____ _____ _____

Answers to these questions can be found on page 75.

15

Session A

7 Summary

- Tough times can have their origins in demands from the nature of the **work** itself, from **people** and from **change**.

- Work itself usually gives rise to **time, mental, emotional** and **physical** demands.

- Work demands often **fluctuate** according to predictable peaks and troughs.

- **Unexpected demands** are especially difficult as they disrupt normal routines and increase the risk of errors.

- Managing the **human demands** of a team is a major source of tough times.

- Other groups whose demands can contribute to tough times are **line managers, customers, family and friends**, and **yourself**.

- Periods of **rapid change**, even when the changes are for the better, can be experienced as tough times.

- The threat of **losing your job** and dealing with **staff who have lost their jobs** is a common feature of tough times.

- Coping with the need to **keep knowledge and skills up-to-date** can be a source of pressure.

- **Changing attitudes** towards authority are a challenge for supervisors and team leaders.

- **Change fatigue** can make it harder to obtain staff commitment.

Session B
How do you cope with tough times?

1 Introduction

> **Stress:** environmental factors which exert an undue strain, or pressure, on a person. This strain can be mental, physical or social and will vary from individual to individual. Definition given by the 'white collar' union ASTMS, now part of MSF.

A supervisor on a course I once ran told how one of his team had come to him. The team member was going through a bad patch in his marriage and this was spilling over into his working life. The supervisor tried to be sympathetic, but his basic message was, 'Pull yourself together'. The team member went home that evening, took a drug overdose and died. He could no longer cope with his tough times. The supervisor was left with the question of how he could have coped better with the situation that was presented to him.

Most tough times do not end quite so tragically. But for very many people tough times mean pain and unhappiness. For some of them tough times mean illness, breakdown, destruction of relationships and loss of job, income and security.

In Session A we looked at the multiple demands that can cause periods of prolonged stress. In this present session we go on to examine how you may react to tough times.

Session B

2 What to look for

2.1 Major triggers

If you are going to help yourself and others in tough times, you can be forewarned if you know which conditions may trigger a tough time and which symptoms people are likely to show when they are experiencing a situation as tough. This experience is usually referred to as 'stress'. In Session A you looked at a wide variety of contributory factors that are more or less persistent features of the working situation. In addition, psychologists have identified a number of specific events that are likely to be experienced as highly stressful.

Activity 13 · 5 mins

Listed below are ten events that are usually stressful. Order these events according to how stressful you think they are. Put a 1 against the event you think is the most stressful, a 2 against the next most stressful, and so on.

- trouble with boss ☐
- divorce ☐
- change in work hours or conditions ☐
- minor violations of the law ☐
- death of spouse ☐
- dismissal from work ☐
- change in responsibilities at work ☐
- sex difficulties ☐
- marriage ☐
- retirement ☐

Session B

You will find feedback on Activity 13 on page 80. What is important to note is that these events have a cumulative effect, especially if they all occur within the same year. For example, if you take on a more demanding job at work you may be able to cope with this without too much difficulty. If, however, within the same twelve-month period you also got married and were charged with a driving offence, then you are likely to show some of the signs of stress that we shall look at shortly.

If you know which events are likely to be stressful, then you may be able to take appropriate action where you can influence some of the events concerned. For example, is it really a good idea to take on a new job, get married, and move house all within six weeks?

2.2 Physical signs of stress

Often the first signs of stress will be some minor physical complaint. Initially, we may not even associate these with the difficult time we are having at work or home.

Activity 14 — 5 mins

Have you experienced any of the following physical problems in the last six months?

- headaches or migraines;
- backache;
- muscle cramps;
- poor sleep;
- indigestion;
- loss of sexual desire;
- persistent tiredness;
- skin problems;
- eye problems (e.g. double vision or difficulty focusing);
- tingling sensations in arms or legs.

Looking back, were these signs connected with any tough time you were having?

_____

_____

_____

Session B

Of course these kinds of problem can be caused by factors other than a tough time. For example, muscle cramps could be caused by unaccustomed exercise, or a skin rash might have been the result of handling some irritating substance. But if you cannot identify any obvious cause of any problem you have had, or if you have had several of these problems around the same time, then it is worthwhile considering whether this is the way your body responds to stress.

2.3 Emotional symptoms

Sometimes you may become aware of stress more through emotional rather than physical symptoms.

Activity 15 · 3 mins

When you are under stress do you notice whether you have any of the following?

- wild swings in mood;
- excessive worries about things that do not really matter;
- over-concern about your health;
- withdrawal and daydreams;
- inability to feel sympathy for others;
- tiredness and lack of concentration;
- increased irritability and anxiety.

When your feelings are upset, it is often difficult at the time to see that anything is wrong. But if you look back at the end of the day, say, you may realize that you were unable to concentrate on work at all. Maybe you found yourself shouting at your children for things you would usually ignore or even find funny. Maybe you were incredibly optimistic and confident one moment, and a few minutes later full of black despair. If you have seen signs like this, take note: it is probable that you are under stress and need to do something about it. These kinds of emotional symptoms are also signs that you should be looking for in the others around you at work.

Session B

2.4 Behavioural symptoms

The third set of symptoms you should watch for are the behavioural signs of stress. You should look for these in yourself, but they are especially valuable in telling you about who in your workplace may be stressed and needing help. Some of the more common behavioural symptoms are:

- indecision;
- complaining unreasonably;
- becoming accident prone;
- driving carelessly;
- poor work;
- drinking more alcohol;
- smoking more;
- increased use of drugs (e.g. tranquillizers, sleeping tablets, illegal drugs);
- eating more than usual (or sometimes eating too little);
- change in sleep pattern; difficulty getting to sleep and waking tired.

3 We are all different

Even when two people are experiencing similar stress, how they react is a very individual affair. One person, for example, may react more with physical symptoms, whereas another person facing the same demands may react with emotional symptoms.

Audrey Livingstone Booth in her book *Stressmanship* describes two high-risk personality types. First is the 'anxious worrier'. This name is fairly self-explanatory and refers to the person who is over-conscientious and has to get every little detail perfect. This type of person is prone to both nervous and physical illness. The other high-risk personality is the 'hot ambitious' type. This person wants to achieve a lot and gets angry and irritated when any difficulty arises. This type is especially prone to physical illness.

EXTENSION 2
You will find a questionnaire in *Stressmanship* by Audrey Livingstone Booth if you want to do a more thorough check on your stress personality type.

Activity 16 · 5 mins

Are you either an anxious worrier or a hot ambitious type? Check your assessment with somebody who knows you well.

21

Session B

In reality, most people are some mixture of these types, although one type will usually dominate. Knowing your dominant type and how high your stress risk is can help you decide if you need to take measures to reduce your reactions to stress and, if so, which kinds of counter-measures will help you most. You can find more about this in Session C.

4 The three stages of stress

Although certain very severe events – for example the unexpected death of a partner – can provoke stress reactions, work-related stress is usually more gradual. It is something that creeps up on us, almost without our realizing, at least in the early days. Audrey Livingstone Booth gives a useful description of three stages of stress.

4.1 Stage I – Mobilizing energy

So far we have talked as if stress is always 'bad'. In fact, stress can be valuable under the right circumstances. The diagram below shows what happens in Stage I stress.

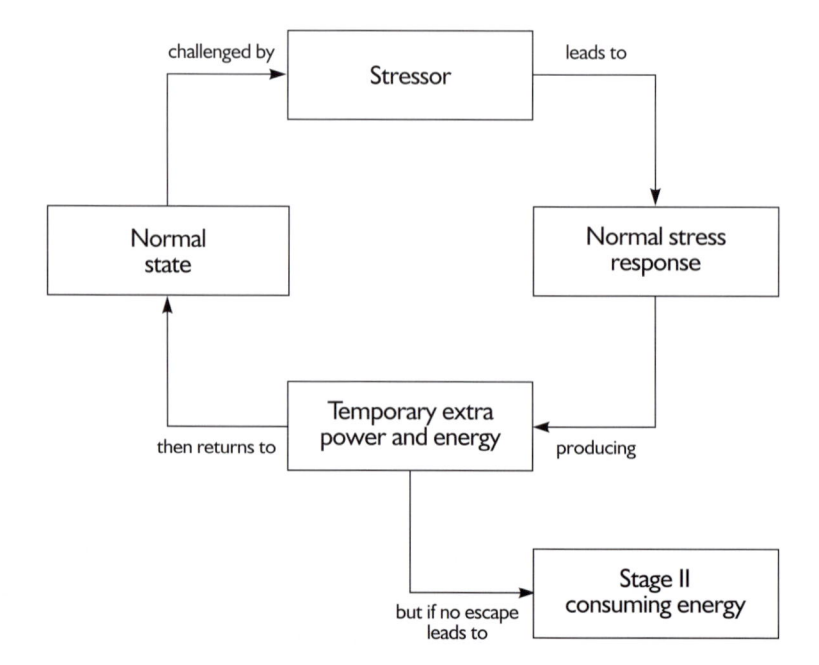

```
                  challenged by      Stressor      leads to
                 ┌──────────────────►        ──────────────┐
                 │                                          ▼
           ┌──────────┐                              ┌──────────────┐
           │  Normal  │                              │ Normal stress│
           │  state   │                              │  response    │
           └──────────┘                              └──────────────┘
                 ▲                                          │
                 │         ┌────────────────────┐           │
                 │         │  Temporary extra   │           │
                 └─────────│  power and energy  │◄──────────┘
                 then returns to └──────────────┘   producing
                                    │
                                    │ but if no escape
                                    │ leads to
                                    ▼
                              ┌──────────────┐
                              │   Stage II   │
                              │consuming energy│
                              └──────────────┘
```

22

Session B

This figure shows that we have a normal 'unstressed' state. When some source of stress arises (the 'stressor'), our bodies react with the normal stress response which includes, among many subtle reactions, the well-known release of adrenalin into our bloodstream. This response is sometimes called the 'fight or flight' reaction, since our bodies prepare to respond to a threat by mobilizing all our energy. Once the threat has been removed (we have fought it and won or run away faster than it could pursue us), then our bodies return to the normal state.

Activity 17

2 mins

How do you feel and act when under Stage I stress?

_____

_____

In this initial state of stress we often feel great. We tend to feel full of energy and able to conquer the world. We walk, talk, eat and think more quickly.

The fight or flight response was fine when it was developed by primitive man and woman, facing threats from, say, sabre-toothed tigers. It is still fine when the threat is identifiable and temporary, such as a deadline to deliver a rush order. But for much of today's working life, the threats are neither well-defined nor temporary. Threats may be a general sense of insecurity. Threats may rapidly follow on each others' heels. Threats may persist. In such cases, there is no return to the normal state. Our bodies stay geared up for drastic action. This takes us to Stage II.

4.2 Stage II – Consuming energy

If the state of stress continues over a longer period of time then our bodies respond by releasing a cocktail of substances into our blood stream, all designed to help us tap into deeper reserves of energy. If these substances are not used up – and nowadays our lifestyles do not encourage us to take the exercise that would help – then our bodies start to show the physical signs of stress we looked at a little earlier. It is not only our bodies, but also our

Session B

emotions and our behaviour, which start to go wrong under the impact of continuing stress. Our decreasing physical, emotional and mental capacities add further to our experience of stress. The diagram below shows what happens.

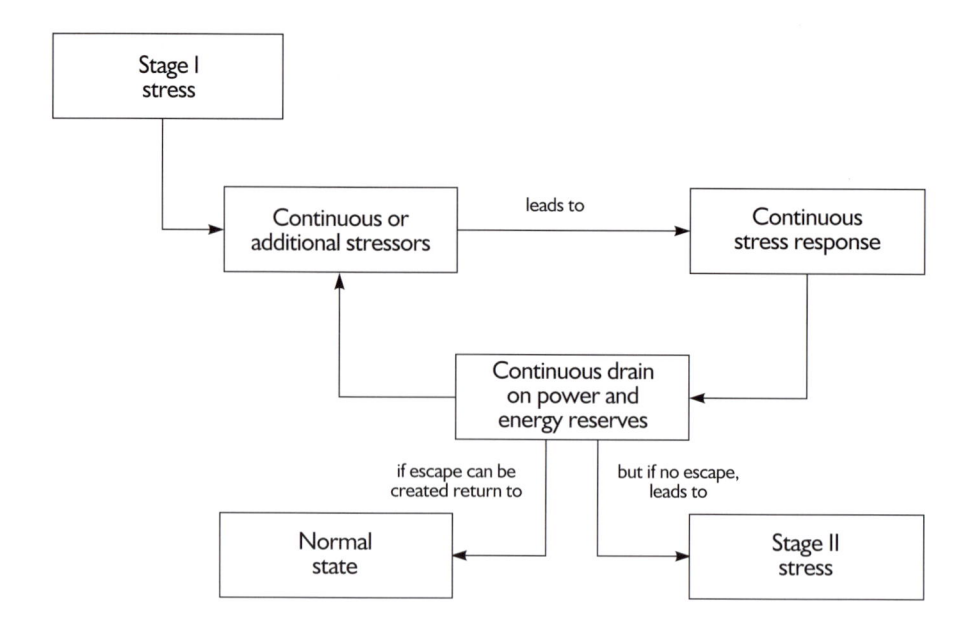

```
         ┌──────────┐
         │ Stage I  │
         │  stress  │
         └────┬─────┘
              │
              ▼
    ┌──────────────────┐   leads to   ┌──────────────────┐
    │  Continuous or   │─────────────▶│   Continuous     │
    │ additional       │              │ stress response  │
    │  stressors       │              │                  │
    └──────────────────┘              └──────────────────┘
              ▲                                │
              │                                │
              │         ┌──────────────┐       │
              │         │ Continuous   │       │
              └─────────│ drain on     │◀──────┘
                        │ power and    │
                        │ energy       │
                        │ reserves     │
                        └──┬────────┬──┘
           if escape can be │        │ but if no escape,
           created return to│        │ leads to
                        ▼            ▼
                  ┌─────────┐   ┌─────────┐
                  │ Normal  │   │ Stage II│
                  │ state   │   │ stress  │
                  └─────────┘   └─────────┘
```

Activity 18 · *2 mins*

How do you feel and act when under Stage II stress?

_____
_____
_____

As we have seen, we all vary in our reactions to increasing stress, but you are now likely to feel driven and under time pressure. You may be tired and anxious. You start to forget things. You may start turning to food, chocolate, alcohol, and other physical comforts.

Once again, if we find a way out of our stress we can return to our normal states without damage, provided the stay in Stage II stress was not too prolonged. If we cannot find an escape route, however, then we are on the way to Stage III stress.

Session B

4.3 Stage III – Draining energy stores

In Stage II stress we are using up energy much faster than we can replace it. This can of course, only go on for so long. A point will be reached where our energy supplies start to run out. One consequence is that our immune system – the complex array of interlocking mechanisms that serve to keep out infection and other physical threats – starts to give way. On top of the decline in our abilities to think, feel and act in appropriate ways, we now start to become really ill. What happens in Stage III stress is shown in the diagram below.

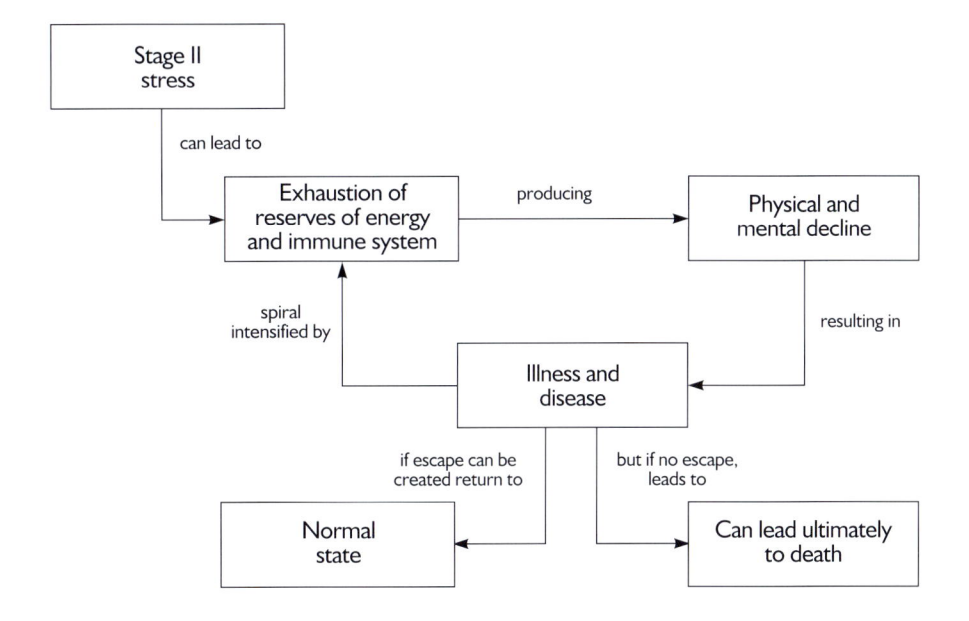

```
     Stage II
      stress
         │
         │ can lead to
         ▼
  Exhaustion of          producing        Physical and
  reserves of energy  ──────────────▶    mental decline
  and immune system                           │
         ▲                                    │ resulting in
         │ spiral                             │
         │ intensified by                     ▼
         │                              Illness and
         └──────────────────────────────  disease
                          ┌─────────────────┴─────────────────┐
                if escape can be                    but if no escape,
                created return to                        leads to
                          ▼                                  ▼
                      Normal      ◀──────────        Can lead ultimately
                       state                              to death
```

The relatively minor physical complaints we listed earlier are now joined by more serious illnesses and medical conditions. Stress-related problems include heart disease, high blood pressure, peptic ulcers, diabetes, dermatitis, asthma, depression and gynaecological problems.

As with the earlier stages, we may still be able to discover a way out, although by now we may be scarred physically or emotionally. If a way out is not found, then breakdown or even death may result, as in the real-life example with which we opened this session.

Session B

Activity 19

30 mins

S/NVQ A1.2

This Activity may provide the basis of appropriate evidence for your S/NVQ portfolio. If you are intending to take this course of action, it might be better to write your answers on separate sheets of paper.

Think of a situation in your life where you were severely stressed. What caused this stress? Try to think of as many different contributing factors at work, home or elsewhere. At your lowest point were you in Stage I, II or III stress? What were your signs of stress? How did you feel? How did you being under stress affect other people around you?

You may find it helpful to talk this activity through with someone you trust and who could help you understand what happened.

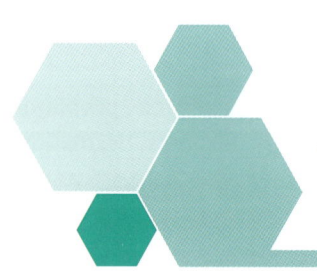

_____
_____
_____
_____
_____
_____

5 How stress can affect your organization

So far we have looked at the kinds of thing that cause stress to people in their personal lives, and how that stress shows itself physically, emotionally and behaviourally.

In this part of the Session we will think about stress in the workplace. We will consider how it affects the organization as a whole and its impact on individuals within the organization. Finally we will look at how stress in the

Session B

workplace can be recognized, its likely causes, and what you can do to alleviate any problems that result.

5.1 Impact of stress on organizations

The success of any organization depends on the effectiveness and commitment of its workforce. Any significant dissatisfaction or resentment among staff caused by stress can have a serious effect both on the overall achievement of the organization and on the way it is seen by others.

So what are the signs that indicate that an organization is being affected by stress in its workforce?

Activity 20 · 10 mins

Write down four indicators that might suggest that an organization is being negatively affected by stress in its workforce.

_____
_____
_____
_____

Your suggestions might have included high levels of absenteeism, lack of motivation, poor-quality work, inter-team and inter-departmental conflict, high staff turnover, lack of pride in the organization.

Of course not all stress has a negative impact. Some of the greatest success stories are of companies in competitive environments where the stress of competition has inspired individuals to achieve great things, and to pull together as a team.

However, more often than not stress is a negative factor in the work environment. And you need to be able to recognize it both in yourself and in your team so that it can be dealt with effectively.

Session B

5.2 Recognizing work-related stress

Work-related stress forms part of a vicious circle. A workforce that is stressed by the working environment will be less efficient or motivated than it would be otherwise. This has a negative impact on the organization itself, with the result that working conditions become even worse. So it is important to be able to recognize such situations and, if possible, put them right.

We have discussed the symptoms of stress earlier in this Session, such as tiredness, lack of concentration, indecision and physical discomfort. Now we need to look at what might cause these symptoms in the workplace.

5.3 Causes of work-related stress

At an individual level, stress can have a variety of work-related causes, including:

- conflict with colleagues;
- lack of training;
- poor working environment, for example poor lighting, too much noise;
- lack of equipment;
- lack of sufficient information to do the job;
- lack of appreciation;
- fatigue brought about by frequent change.

At the organizational level, causes of stress can include:

- threat of redundancy;
- failure of management to listen;
- poor corporate image.

Activity 21

10 mins

Think about your own stress at work. Why is it happening? Try to make a list of the causes in the columns below, listing personal causes and work-related causes separately.

Personal causes	Work-related causes
_____	_____
_____	_____
_____	_____
_____	_____

Session B

5.4 Dealing with work-related stress

If someone is regularly absent, has mood swings, or produces consistently poor work, it may be an indication of personal problems, or it may be the result of something being wrong at work. In either case, you should think about what steps you could take to help, either by counselling, referral to expert support groups or, if it is a work-related problem, by taking practical steps to solve it.

Activity 22
12 mins

Make a list of three instances when stress has affected the way one of your team members has been working. Then note down what you think might have been the causes of the stress. Finally, explain how you dealt with the situation and how, in hindsight, you might have handled it differently.

Situation 1
How the stress affected the team member's work:

_____

The causes of the stress were:

_____

You handled it by:

_____

You could have handled it better by:

_____

Situation 2
How the stress affected the team member's work:

_____

The causes of the stress were:

_____

You handled it by:

_____

Session B

You could have handled it better by:

___

Situation 3
How the stress affected the team member's work:

___

The causes of the stress were:

___

You handled it by:

___

You could have handled it better by:

___

Now, finally, look at the list of your own causes of stress that you made in Activity 21. Tick the causes that you can do something about, and make a mental note to try to improve the situation as soon as is practicable.

Next time a member of your team shows signs of stress, follow the steps you took in this last activity. You may find that, by analysing the situation in a more organized way, you will be able to find more effective solutions to the problem.

Self-assessment 2

10 mins

Complete questions 1 to 6.

1 What are the three most common stressful events at work?

___
___
___

Session B

2 List three examples of each kind of stress symptom.

Physical	Emotional	Behavioural

3 What are the two personality types most at risk from stress?

4 What is the name of the reaction when our bodies prepare to respond to stress?

5 What happens to energy in Stage II of stress?

6 List three examples of stress-related illnesses that may appear at Stage III of stress.

7 List three causes of work-related stress.

Answers to these questions can be found on pages 76–7.

Session B

6 Summary

- Many **life events** at work and home, even good ones, increase the risk of suffering from stress.

- The **impact** of stressful life events **accumulates**, so that a number of small to moderate events occurring close together can lead to signs of stress.

- Stress can cause a variety of **physical complaints**, from the merely irritating through to the life-threatening.

- Changes in a person's **emotional** state, especially when coupled with bad or erratic behaviour, can be warning signs of stress.

- People vary widely in how they react to similar stress-inducing circumstances.

- In **Stage I** stress, energy is mobilized; in **Stage II**, energy is consumed; in **Stage III**, energy stores are drained.

- Stress can be caused either by personal circumstances or by the work environment.

Session C
Helping yourself in tough times

1 Introduction

> 'My centre is giving way, my right is in retreat. Situation excellent. I shall attack.' General Foch, Battle of the Marne, 8 September 1914.

The old saying goes, 'when the going gets tough, the tough get going'. Most of us have come across individuals who seem to be at their best in a crisis. The worse the situation becomes, the more they seem confident and in control. Are these people simply born with special gifts? Or have they developed the qualities of toughness and confidence through their own efforts? The view that we take in this third session is that we can all take steps to develop our skills and inner resources, so that when the situation demands more from us, we have more to give.

2 First aid

EXTENSION 3
You will find many more suggestions in the book by Livingstone Booth we have already mentioned (Extension 2); another good book is *Stress at Work* by Joanna Gutman.

When you are in the middle of a tough time there are a great many things you **can do** to help yourself manage better. There are also some things you **should not do**. We look now at some of the things you can do or should not do.

Session C

2.1 Relaxation techniques

There are many techniques for helping us to relax. Here are two. The first is for 'emergency relaxation'[1]

1 Say 'stop' to yourself.

2 Breathe in deeply and breathe out slowly. As you do so, drop your shoulders and relax your hands.

3 Breathe in deeply again – as you breathe out, make sure your teeth aren't held tightly together.

4 Take two small quiet breaths.

Activity 23 · 2 mins

Look for opportunities to try out the emergency relaxation technique. Note down how it helped.

_____

_____

Being able to relax in an emergency is a skill and, like all skills, you may need to practise a number of times before it starts to help. Very soon, you should be able to prevent or at least slow down your stress reactions. This technique is for when you are really under pressure and have no opportunity for anything more elaborate. The second technique is for when you have a chance to try to relax more deeply.[2]

1 Sit quietly in a comfortable position.

2 Close your eyes.

3 Deeply relax all your muscles, beginning at your feet and progressing up to your face. Keep them relaxed.

[1] Madders, J. *Stress and Relaxation*. Third Edition, Dunitz, 1981.
[2] Benson, H. *The Relaxation Response*. Collins, 1976.

Session C

4   Breathe in through your nose. Become aware of your breathing. As you breathe out, say the word 'one' silently to yourself. For example, breathe in ... out, 'one'; in ... out, 'one', and so on. Breathe easily and naturally.

5   Continue for ten to twenty minutes. You may open your eyes to check the time, but do not use an alarm. When you finish, sit quietly for several minutes, at first with your eyes closed and later with your eyes open. Do not stand up for a few minutes.

6   Do not worry about whether you are successful in achieving a deep level of relaxation. Maintain a passive attitude and permit relaxation to occur at its own pace. When distracting thoughts occur, try to ignore them by not dwelling on them and return to repeating 'one'.

It is a good idea to practise relaxation regularly, even when you are not especially under stress. The more you practise, the more skilled you get. You can then readily call on your relaxation skills when you most need them. Once you have developed your relaxation skills, you may be able to help others at work who would also benefit from these techniques.

Activity 24

15 mins

Try out Benson's relaxation method. Try to observe how you feel before and after.

2.2 Minimizing worry

If you are an anxious worrier you may find that you spend your time going over and over a problem without ever finding a solution. However, by using certain simple techniques you can harness your own nervous energy and the experience of other people to move the problem forward.

Here are some ideas for breaking that 'worry' loop.

- Share your worries with people who know you and/or your problem well. The simple action of explaining it can often clarify the problem in your mind and put it more into proportion.
- Write the worry down, then jot down all the solutions you can think of. It doesn't matter how impractical they are at this stage. When you have written

Session C

down all the ideas you can come up with, go over them and cross out the ones that you are sure won't work. Make a list of all the remaining solutions, and make notes on how they might work, who could help you and what the likely outcome might be. Finally, draw up a plan of action based on the most promising solution.

- Take some physical exercise. Any exercise is beneficial, whether it is going for a walk, visiting the gym, playing a game of tennis or football, or even cleaning out the garage. The activity will clear your head and will make you feel more positive and in control of your situation.
- Make a list of all the good aspects of the worry and all the bad aspects. You may find that the good actually outweigh the bad, and that the worry isn't all that significant after all.
- Finally, try some visualization to get everything in proportion. Picture yourself next month or next year, and ask yourself whether your worry will still seem so important. Imagine the worst that could really happen and ask yourself whether this is likely, and whether it would really be so dreadful.

Activity 25

12 mins

Choose one of the techniques we have just discussed, and apply it to a worry that you have got at the moment. Then choose another of the techniques and do the same thing. Then think about how each approach helped you, and what technique you might try next time.

2.3 Releasing anger

Tough times often bring strong feelings of anger. This is especially likely if you consider yourself the hot ambitious type. It is important to find ways to release this anger before it bursts out uncontrollably. Here are some ways you can do this. Get away from everyone and let your anger out verbally or physically but harmlessly. Take a brisk walk. Use the energy of your anger to do some job you have been putting off, and note how the anger has led to you achieving something positive. If being kept waiting makes you angry, take something with you that you want to read when you think you might be delayed.

EXTENSION 2
You can find more about these and other techniques for releasing anger in the book by Audrey Livingstone Booth.

Session C

Activity 26

10 mins

Janice runs a busy travel agency. Her staff think she is something of a perfectionist. Everything must always go exactly to plan and she is not tolerant of mistakes. One day, during a busy time of the year, Janice found everything going wrong. A client came in to complain that his tickets had been booked for the wrong dates. The new member of staff was having trouble finding her way through the catalogues and timetables and kept asking for help. The coffee had run out and nobody had had time to go out and get some more. When Janice's computer screen gave the message, 'Sorry, I am unable to deal with your query right now, please wait', while she was dealing with a customer who kept changing her mind and the new assistant asked for help once more, Janice exploded, questioning the assistant's competence in forthright terms and being rude to the customer about her failure to make her mind up. The assistant was upset, the customer offended, and Janice, when she cooled down, appalled at what she had done.

How do you think Janice could have handled this situation better?

___
___
___
___
___

In my view Janice needed to see how the situation was developing much earlier. The most important thing was that she needed to sense that her anger was building up. Probably the best thing she could have done was to get out of the office for a time, at least withdrawing to the backroom for a while, asking one of the more experienced members of staff to take charge. This might have meant clients had to wait longer or queries that only Janice could answer would have to be dealt with later. Janice might have been concerned about her staff's reaction to her leaving. But all these problems would have been fairly minor compared with what actually happened.

Session C

2.4 Time management and delegation

As we discussed earlier, tough times are usually associated with time pressure. Skills in time management and delegation are essential for today's supervisor/team leader. You can find more in *Managing Time* and *Delegating Effectively* in this series.

2.5 Using your informal support network

Most of us have friends, family and colleagues who can help us – if only we ask. Often we do not ask.

Activity 27 · 5 mins

In the last three months have you asked anybody for help? Who did you ask? What did you ask for? How did they react?

Who else could you ask for help? What kind of help could they offer? Would you feel free to ask? If you have any doubts about asking the person, do these doubts say more about you than about them?

_____
_____
_____
_____
_____

We think other people are too busy, have enough worries themselves, won't put themselves out to help us, and so on. In fact most people are pleased to help if they can, but you must be clear and realistic about the kind of help each person can offer. Some people can provide information or advice. Others can provide practical help, perhaps taking some jobs off us for a time; others can provide moral support. It can be a great help simply knowing someone has taken the time to really listen to our problems.

2.6 Using formal support

In addition to the informal support that you may get from family and friends, there is a whole network of professional organizations and groups available to help you in times of stress. These are discussed in more detail in section 3.3 Counselling (see below).

2.7 Keeping fit

As the three stages of stress make clear, tough times can attack us mentally, emotionally and physically. Being reasonably fit physically equips us to resist attacks on all these levels. The fitter we are the longer we can stay in Stage I where stress can be productive, without sliding towards Stage II or even Stage III. Taking time to relax, eating properly, and getting exercise are essential to staying fit. The trouble is that when we feel under pressure, we let all these go. For a day or two, these kinds of sacrifice are often necessary to meet a particular pressure at work, but if they become your standard way of living and working, then trouble is being stored up.

2.8 Smoking, drink and drugs

In the short term, smoking, drink and drugs may help. But in the longer term, excessive use of any of these substances reduces physical and mental capacities, encouraging the decline from Stage I stress to Stage II and on to Stage III.

2.9 Getting away

We do not like to admit it, but few of us are totally indispensable. Taking a few days' leave, or better still a fortnight's holiday, can help you regain a sense of proportion. Of course most of the problems that were there when you went away will still be there when you return, but you will be able to be more objective about them. You can see which are trivial in reality and can be ignored or dealt with later, and which are important and truly need you to address them.

Session C

Activity 28

30 mins

S/NVQ A1.2

This Activity may provide the basis of appropriate evidence for your S/NVQ portfolio. If you are intending to take this course of action, it might be better to write your answers on separate sheets of paper.

1 Make a list of your main stress reactions you would like to reduce.

2 Make a list of a daily or weekly programme of actions you will take to help reduce your stress reactions (e.g. learn a relaxation technique and practise it for fifteen minutes daily; take at least one full day off each week; reduce smoking and coffee drinking; exercise for thirty minutes at least three times a week).

3 Decide the minimum time for which you will try this programme (suggested minimum: four weeks).

4 Set time aside each week to note down how consistently you have followed your programme, whether your stress reactions are better or worse, and what effect there has been on your performance at work.

5 At the end of your trial period, note down the main results of your programme and how you will now go on (e.g. learn new techniques; drop actions that did not help; increase time given to relaxation/time off/exercise; etc.).

Session C

3 Preparing for tough times

3.1 Being forewarned

Tough times are always worse when they take us by surprise. If we can see the tough time coming, then we can prepare ourselves. Usually there are warning signs – some clues that we could have detected if we had kept our eyes and ears open. For example, redundancy is a blow that often comes as an unexpected shock. But falling orders, reduction in overtime, declining financial performance, changes in top management, and interest from other companies looking for acquisitions are all examples of clues that may signal a tough time is coming.

Sometimes it may be possible to react to these warnings, by taking practical steps. In the case of threats of redundancy, it may be possible to explore other opportunities within the company or elsewhere. It may be possible to put off taking on new financial commitments or other major life changes, as we discussed in Session B.

Perhaps the greatest value of being forewarned is having the time to prepare yourself mentally and emotionally for what may happen. Then you are not knocked off balance. You can keep a cool head and your ideas and actions, when the blow actually comes, are more likely to be appropriate and effective.

Activity 29 *3 mins*

What can you do to keep yourself well-informed about possible tough times?

_____
_____
_____
_____

Session C

Here are some ways to find out what is going on that might turn into a tough time:

- Build up a network of people you talk to regularly (in your company, customers, suppliers, even competitors).
- Follow the economic and business news in the papers and on television and radio.
- Get hold of your company's annual report and press releases.
- Browse the specialist magazines and journals in your sector.
- Go to exhibitions and conferences to keep in touch with trends and rumours.

3.2 Future-proofing your skills

In Session A we looked at changes which may mean that your skills are no longer sufficient to meet the demands of tomorrow's working life. One of the best ways you can help yourself and your staff avoid tough times is to take every opportunity to keep your skills up-to-date.

Activity 30 — 10 mins

Which skills do you think you need to develop to meet the working demands of the coming years? How do you think you can develop these skills?

_____
_____
_____

As we discussed above, keeping skills up-to-date means that you have to monitor trends so that you know what skills are going to be required. The most obvious example of recent years has been the need to develop skills in using personal computers. Nowadays anyone who wants to work in an office-based job, but does not know how to use a PC for basic office tasks is unlikely to find work. Changes in working practices mean that people are more likely to need good teamwork and communication skills. You can probably identify other skills that are going to be more and more important for your particular line of work.

Your training department and local college should be able to help you here. It is advisable to keep in regular contact with them.

Session C

3.3 Belief in what you do

There is plenty of evidence that people who believe in what they are doing are much better able to withstand the stresses and strains of tough times. If you believe that your work is 'pointless' or 'a waste of time', then you will experience even a few minor difficulties as a real tough time. You will soon want to give up. In contrast, if you believe that what you are doing is important and worth doing, then even the biggest problems may seem to you a price worth paying.

This is a matter of your personal values – those things that you consider good, right and proper. For example, if you are expected to tell lies in your work (e.g. 'the cheque is in the post') and you consider this immoral, then your work and values are in conflict. Similarly, if you attach great importance to the environment and you think your company's products are damaging to the environment, then you are going to experience discomfort at the least.

Belief in what you do can also involve your own ambitions. If you have always wanted an outdoor job and are working in an office, you may be less than fully committed to your work. Or if you consider your present job does not fully use all your knowledge, skills and talents, your sense of frustration and disappointment will contribute to your experience of tough times.

Activity 31   3 mins

Answer yes or no to the following questions:

1 Is the work you do consistent with your personal values?   Yes/No

2 Does your job use you to your full potential?   Yes/No

If you answered yes to both questions, then you are probably in the right job for you. Things will have to get very bad before you experience them as tough times. If you answered no to both questions, then you are probably in the wrong job. It will not take too many difficulties before you experience a tough time. It is probably worth exploring with someone you trust what future direction your career should take.

Session C

If you answered no to one question, then either you are doing work with which you do not fully agree or you feel your talents are not being used properly. Either way, you are likely to suffer from less than total commitment. It is likely to be worthwhile talking your situation through with an experienced careers adviser.

3.4 When it all goes wrong

Failures are well-known parts of the background of star performers, those promoted several times. They talk openly and regularly about 'my biggest embarrassment,' 'my top ten foul-ups . . .' (while making it clear that they kept on trying until they got it right).[1]

There will be occasions when, in spite of all your care and preparations, everything does go completely wrong. Sometimes you will fail. For most people, failure on any significant scale equals a tough time. Your attitudes to failure are all-important.

Activity 32 · 3 mins

Answer yes or no to the following questions:

1 Do you think failure should never happen?   Yes/No

2 Do you look for someone else to blame when you fail?   Yes/No

3 Does a failure send you into deep despair?   Yes/No

4 Do you try to hide your failures?   Yes/No

If you answered yes to most of these questions, you probably need to take a deeper look at your attitudes to failure, especially if the failure is the result of a well-planned good try at something, which nonetheless went wrong. In these cases the right question is not 'who to blame', but 'what can be learned from this failure'.

[1] Peters, T. and Austin, N. *A Passion for Excellence*, page 194. Fontana 1986.

Session C

Without mistakes and failures there is no learning. Somebody once said that the only real failures are those from which nothing is learned. There is no time so tough that something positive cannot be rescued from it by asking 'what have I learned from all this?'. By ourselves it is often difficult to be objective about our failures. Here it can be helpful to find a 'mentor' – someone who has an understanding of you and your work (although they need not necessarily work with you). A good mentor is someone who you can talk to. They will not judge you, but will help you learn from what has happened. We will look briefly at what mentoring involves in Session D.

Self-assessment 3

10 mins

1 Which of the following statements are good advice to somebody suffering from stress?

 a Take time out to relax.
 b Take your worries very seriously.
 c Keep your anger bottled up.
 d Develop your time management skills.
 e Do everything yourself.
 f Ask friends, family and colleagues for help.
 g Take as much physical exercise as you can.
 h Keep your alcohol consumption moderate.
 i Never take time off when the pressure is on.

2 List three ways you may be able to predict tough times before they happen:

_____

_____

_____

For the remaining questions, complete the sentences with a suitable word or words from following list:

MENTOR	FIT	FAILURES
VALUES	RELAX	TRAINING
NETWORK	AMBITIONS	RELEASE

45

Session C

3 If you are an anxious worrier you need to learn techniques to help you _____.

4 If you are a hot ambitious type you need to find ways to _____ your anger.

5 Keeping _____ is important in protecting yourself against stress.

6 A _____ made up of colleagues, friends and family can be an important source of support in tough times.

7 To keep your skills future-proofed you need _____.

8 There is always an opportunity to learn, even from the worst of _____.

9 A _____ is someone who can help you learn from your experiences.

10 Belief in your work is strongest when your job is consistent with your _____ and _____.

Answers to these questions can be found on pages 77–8.

4 Summary

- **Emergency relaxation** can help you when you are in the middle of a difficult situation.

- Techniques for deeper relaxation can help counter the harmful effects of stress.

- There are techniques for helping to **minimize worry** and **release anger**.

- **Time management** and **delegation** can help prevent stressful situations building up.

- It is advisable to build up **an informal network** of colleagues, family and friends who can provide practical and moral support in tough times.

- **Exercising** to keep at least a basic level of fitness is a wise precaution against stress.

- Smoking, alcohol and drugs **reduce resistance** to stress in the long run.

- **Taking a break** from work can restore a sense of perspective which can help you cope with tough times.

- **Keeping yourself informed** about developments or events that may indicate a tough time is coming is important so that you can be emotionally prepared and, where possible, take preventive action.

- **Continuing training** can help ensure that your knowledge and skills do not become out-of-date.

- Tough times are easier to bear if your work is consistent with your **values** and **ambitions**.

- Failures are always **opportunities to learn**, although help from a **mentor** may be needed to find what can be learned.

Session D
Helping others in tough times

1 Introduction

As a first line manager, you are responsible not only for coping with your own tough times, but also for helping your team members with the tough times they may be experiencing at work. All of the techniques you looked at in Session C may be helpful to others. You should, for example, forewarn your team of likely difficult times ahead, help them keep their skills up-to-date, and work with them to learn from failures. In addition, there are some specific kinds of help you may be able to provide through your role as a first line manager.

2 Promoting teamwork

Probably the most common cause of tough times is excessive demands from the working situation. One of the best defences against this is teamwork, but your workteam must be a genuine team, not merely a group of individuals who happen to work together. Real teams provide moral support to each other, as well as practical help.

At the practical level, where the problem is the size of the workload, you can of course help the team by ensuring that, as far as possible, the load is spread evenly so that one or two individuals are not carrying an unfair share of the burden. But it is even better if you can develop your team so that the team members have the skills and flexible ways of working that enable them to allocate the work in the best way themselves. By helping your staff become a real team, you will all be able to cope better with tough times.

Session D

Activity 33 — 10 mins

On the basis of your experience with your workteam, assess the level of teamwork by answering the following questions yes or no.

1 Do the members of your team see themselves as a team whose success depends on them all working together? Yes/No

2 Do the members of your team tend to have the same views on what is important? Yes/No

3 Do the members of your team understand the working of the whole team well enough to know what the consequences of their own actions will be for the others? Yes/No

4 Do the members of your team have the knowledge and skills to help each other? Yes/No

5 Are the members of your team willing to help each other? Yes/No

6 Do members of your team keep an eye on each other so they know when somebody needs help? Yes/No

7 Are the team's ways of working sufficiently flexible that team members can reorganize themselves to meet changing work demands? Yes/No

8 Do members of your team have good enough communication skills that they reliably know what each other means? Yes/No

9 Do team members trust each other enough to be open about their needs and to give each other constructive feedback, knowing that this will be accepted? Yes/No

10 Do members of your team try to find ways of improving their working together as a team? Yes/No

If you answered no to any of these questions, then this points to an area where you may be able to improve teamwork. It is beyond the scope of this workbook to go fully into team building, but two other workbooks in this series (*Leading your Team* and *Working in Teams*) provide detailed coverage of this issue.

Session D

When planning work for your team, try to build sensible contingencies into it: allowances of time or money to cater for things going wrong, taking longer or costing more than expected. Follow the maxim: 'Hope for the best, but plan for the worst'.

3 Supporting and advising, counselling and mentoring

There are a number of ways in which you can provide help to members of your team in tough times. The main techniques you will find useful are:

- supporting and advising;
- counselling;
- mentoring.

3.1 Supporting and advising

You can support the members of your team by giving practical help when a problem arises. This can very often occur as a result of the 'ripple' effect of change elsewhere in the organization.

One of the most common situations when your support and advice are needed is during an organizational change resulting in redundancy.

It may happen that one or more members of your team are made redundant and you may find yourself having to help them cope. You are likely to find this a sensitive matter, since others are losing their jobs while you are keeping yours. Depending on how the redundancies are being managed you may be able to use your influence to help those being made redundant. You may perhaps be able to ensure that:

- the news of redundancy is not announced on some special day for them, such as their birthday;
- they are given a definite date for them to leave, so that they can plan ahead;
- where somebody has a company car, you could arrange for it to be available for a while, for use as needed;
- things like medical insurance cover are maintained for a time.

Session D

Activity 34

2 mins

How do you think somebody being made redundant feels? How should you deal with these feelings?

_____
_____
_____

If you are trying to help someone who has just been made redundant, you must expect the person to be angry. You will probably not be able to deal with practicalities until the person has expressed their feelings. It may be advisable to deal with this early on, asking the person how they are feeling. While they express their anger, it is probably best just to listen, not to sympathize or be defensive. When they have finished, simply acknowledge their anger.

If you think the person has a reasonable chance of finding another job, then you can talk through possible directions with them. If you think the person is unlikely to find a job with another company, you can discuss possibilities of early retirement, part-time work, or maybe self-employment. In all cases you should make sure that they are getting the help they need from your personnel or human resources department, or from specialist consultants, if your company has provided such a service.

Activity 35

5 mins

You will also have to keep dealing with the rest of the team who have not been made redundant. Note down how you think they are likely to feel.

_____
_____
_____
_____
_____

Session D

John McManus in his book *The Perfect Dismissal*[1] suggests the survivors of redundancy may feel:

- **guilt** – at having survived;

- **jealousy** – they'll be aware that some attractive settlements have been made, and some of the people involved will walk straight into new jobs;

- **fear** – wondering when it is going to be their turn;

- **outrage** – there didn't seem to be much fairness or even sense in the selection criteria for redundancy;

- **mistrust** – management cannot now be trusted, whatever they say;

- **inadequacy** – the extent and requirements of individual jobs have been increased (Can they cope?);

- **culture shock** – the company culture has changed dramatically (Will they like the new one? Can they survive it?).

3.2 Counselling

There may be occasions when you see that a personal problem is affecting the work of one of your team and you need to help. Sometimes team members may themselves say that they want to talk to you about some problem that is troubling them.

Counselling is a one-to-one activity in which one person helps another to help himself or herself. Counselling helps people who are being counselled to:
- explore their feelings, thoughts and actions;
- reach a better understanding of themselves;
- make appropriate decisions or take relevant action.

In arranging such a counselling session, remember that the other person is likely to want privacy and your close attention. Choose a time when you will have a reasonable period to talk privately and free from interruptions. Arrange for somebody else to take your phone calls. Do not sit on either side of a desk or table. Try to find a more informal, comfortable setting and arrange the chairs so that you are not directly facing each other – this makes it natural and easy not to look straight at each other, which can be intimidating when discussing sensitive issues.

[1] McManus, J. *The Perfect Dismissal*, Century Business, 1993.

Session D

The golden rule in helping people with personal problems is that only they can solve their problems. It is not your job to solve the problems for them and you probably would not succeed even if you tried. So do not try to give them a 'solution'. Similarly, giving lots of 'good advice' is usually counter-productive, as you may have experienced yourself.

In many situations the best assistance you can provide is to help those concerned define the problem that is troubling them. Often people are unclear about what exactly is the matter. Often what they see as the problem (e.g. drinking too much) is only a symptom of a deeper problem (e.g. a relationship problem or dissatisfaction in their job). Your role is simply to try to understand. Questioning and listening skills are important here. Ask questions simply to help you understand. Show actively that you are listening by your attention, by the kinds of question you ask, and by checking to see you have understood correctly what the other person has said.

Remarkably often this is all that the person requires. By coming to a clear recognition of their problem and, importantly, accepting that they do indeed have a problem, the person may be able to go away and tackle it themselves without further help. If this is not enough, however, you may have to go on to help the other person redefine the problem. Many problems are caused, or at least made worse, by the way in which people define them. They become stuck, only able to see the problem from one point of view. Your role now is to challenge the way people see their problems. If they can come to see their problem from another perspective, then ways for solving the problem often become clearer. Challenging does not usually mean confronting. It often means asking questions that will help the person to see the limited view they are taking of the problem and to consider other angles.

If you can help the other person do this, they should now have a fresh outlook on their problem and broad ideas about what to do. You can then go on to help the other person look at the options open to them, seeing where he or she might need more help or information, and working out a plan of action. As the person's supervisor or team leader, there may be certain practical things that you have to do to help the other person carry out his or her plan.

Whenever you become involved in counselling a member of your team, you must treat it in complete confidentiality. At no time should you involve third parties without obtaining the permission of the person you are counselling.

Session D

Activity 36

30 mins

S/NVQ C15.1

This Activity (which is also relevant to the Personal Competence building teams) may provide the basis of appropriate evidence for your S/NVQ portfolio. If you are intending to take this course of action, it might be better to write your answers on separate sheets of paper.

Write brief answers to each of the following questions about an experience you have had helping somebody with a personal problem. Make sure that the identity of the person concerned is not recognizable from what you write. Use a situation from your working life if possible. If you have not had an appropriate example connected with your work, choose an example from outside work.

1 What was the situation, who was the person (indicate only as team member X, a friend, etc.) and what was their problem?

2 How was the problem affecting the person?

3 How did you become aware of the problem?

4 Where, when and how did you try to help?

Session D

5 What measures did you take to respect the other person's privacy and feelings?

6 Did you try to help the other person find his or her own solution?

7 Did the other person appear to get what he or she wanted from your help?

8 What, if anything, would you do differently now?

EXTENSIONS 4 and 5
If helping people with personal problems is a task you often find yourself undertaking, you may find it useful to read the books by Reddy (Extension 4) and De Board (Extension 5).

As a final word of caution, it is important to be aware of your own limitations in helping others deal with personal problems. Always ask yourself whether this is a problem you are competent to help with. If you are in the process of trying to help, recognize that there may come a stage when you should stop and suggest the other person seeks more specialist guidance.

There are many professional sources of information and advice available to anyone who needs them, many of them free. They include:

- local authority and government information services;
- local authority housing departments;
- professional stress counsellors;
- local solicitors.

National organizations run on a charitable basis include:

- Samaritans;
- Alcoholics Anonymous;

Session D

- Citizens' Advice Bureaux;
- Relate;
- Gingerbread Advice Line for Lone Parents;
- NHS Direct;
- Refuge Domestic Violence Helpline;
- Shelter.

Activity 37 · *12 mins*

Obtain a copy of Yellow Pages and find the section on Helplines at the beginning of the book. There may be situations in the future where knowing where to look for expert advice will be of great help to one of the members of your team. Yellow Pages is also available on-line.

3.3 Mentoring

The *Concise Oxford Dictionary* defines a mentor as 'an experienced and trusted advisor'.

Mentoring has been used for centuries as a means of passing on experience and wisdom to younger generations. It was the cornerstone of the guild apprentice system in which master craftsmen were responsible for developing the skills of their apprentices in a particular trade. Mentoring has also existed in less formal ways, for instance through managers taking younger members of staff 'under their wing', so that they can successfully develop their careers in the organization.

You can learn more about mentoring in *Delivering Training*.

Session D

Self-assessment 4

10 mins

For questions 1 to 6 complete the sentences with a suitable word or words chosen from the following list:

| DEFINE | FEAR | WORST | PERSONAL |
| TEAMWORK | ANGER | BEST | GUILT |

1 Helping each other in tough times requires _____.

2 Hope for the _____ but plan for the _____.

3 The main emotion of someone who has been made redundant is likely to be _____.

4 Two common feelings of survivors of redundancy are _____ and _____.

5 A person's _____ problems can sometimes affect their performance at work.

6 With many problems a person just needs somebody else to help them _____ the real nature of the problem.

7 Which of the following statements are good advice to a supervisor or team leader helping team members in tough times?

   a Encourage your team members to look after 'number one'. ☐

   b Help your team find flexible ways of working. ☐

   c When planning, always assume the best will happen. ☐

   d Take care to keep your own skills and those of your team up-to-date. ☐

   e There is nothing much you can do to help with something as bad as redundancy. ☐

   f When dealing with redundancy, remember the survivors need help too. ☐

   g Never get involved in a team member's personal problems. ☐

   h When helping somebody with a personal problem, give them lots of good advice. ☐

   i Find out the most appropriate source of specialist help if you think you yourself cannot help. ☐

Answers to these questions can be found on page 78.

4 Summary

- In tough times, teams can give each other both **practical** and **moral support**.

- Build **contingencies** into plans to allow for the unexpected.

- You can help members of your team to cope with problems through **supporting** and **advising**, **counselling** and **mentoring**.

- **Care** and **forethought** can help make redundancy no worse than it need be.

- It is difficult to help people who have been made redundant until they have had a chance to express their **anger**.

- **Survivors of redundancy** will need help too.

- Only the person with a personal problem can solve that problem.

- When helping with personal problems, avoid giving 'solutions' and 'good advice'.

- In helping with personal problems, simply **listening** and trying to **understand** can help a person define the true problem. This may often be all the help they need.

- There will be occasions when **specialist outside help** is needed.

Performance checks

1 Quick quiz

Jot down the answers to the following questions on *Managing Tough Times*.

Question 1 When feelings of stress, fear and threat persist what are you likely to experience?

_____

Question 2 Name the four kinds of work-related demands that we discussed in the workbook.

_____
_____
_____
_____

Question 3 Name the five groups of people whose demands often contribute to pressure at work.

_____
_____
_____
_____
_____

Performance checks

Question 4 How have the jobs of many first line managers changed in ways that might add to their feelings of being under pressure?

Question 5 How might rapidly changing technology contribute to a person's experience of a tough time?

Question 6 What is the most stressful event connected with working life?

Question 7 Give three examples of physical complaints that can be caused by stress.

Question 8 As well as physical symptoms, what other kinds of stress symptoms should you look out for?

Question 9 Which types of people are most at risk from stress?

Question 10 Describe the three phases of stress in terms of what happens to a person's energy.

Performance checks

Question 11 Give three examples of measures you can take to reduce the effects of stress.

Question 12 Why does being aware early of likely threats or difficulties help cope with tough times?

Question 13 How can you gain something of value from even the worst of failures?

Question 14 How can teamwork help people cope with tough times?

Question 15 List three concerns of people who have not been made redundant when others around them have.

Question 16 How does counselling differ from mentoring?

Answers to these questions can be found on pages 78–80.

Performance checks

2 Workbook assessment

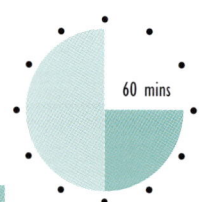

60 mins

Read the following case of someone having a tough time at work and then answer the questions below, writing your answers on a separate sheet of paper.

> John is a supervisor working for an electricity distribution company. He leads a team of technicians who maintain distribution equipment. He has always liked his job. It has been a source of pride to him that he and his team could deal with all the problems life brings, such as having to turn out at midnight in foul weather to deal with an emergency.
>
> Lately, however, it has all begun to get too much. His team has just started a complicated maintenance job that requires a lot of overtime. He is having to spend a lot of time on top of his normal work documenting procedures for his section's new quality manual. His wife is complaining about how little time he spends at home with his family. The new area manager is being difficult, changing a lot of working practices that have been agreed for years. John is worried about allegations that one of his workteam has started drinking heavily at lunch times. John fears that the standard of this person's work may drop, putting the safety of the systems at risk.
>
> At a time when he feels he is really needed more than full time at the depot, John has been told that he has to go on a week's course to learn about new computer-based control systems. On top of all this, rumours about a possible takeover have made John and his colleagues ask a lot of questions about their future job security.
>
> The everyday working difficulties that normally John would have taken in his stride, have started to loom as major problems. He has found himself shouting at members of his team. His paperwork is getting way behind. He can see no way of improving the situation.

Write down:

- what you think John's most urgent task is;
- how you think he should take hold of the situation in the short term;
- what actions you think he should take to improve the situation in the long term.

Performance checks

Give the reasons behind your thinking.

You can make any assumptions about the work or the organization that seem reasonable (e.g. other members of the team; sources of help that may be available).

3 Work-based assignment

S/NVQs A1.2, C15.1

The time guide for this assignment gives you an approximate idea of how long it is likely to take you to write up your findings. You will find you need to spend some additional time gathering information, perhaps talking to colleagues and thinking about the assignment. The results of your efforts should be presented on separate sheets of paper.

This assignment may provide the basis of appropriate evidence for your S/NVQ portfolio. The assignment is designed to help you demonstrate:

- your ability to identify situations that are likely to be very demanding for you and your team;
- your ability to recognize the signs of stress in yourself;
- your ability to recognize the signs of stress in others;
- your ability to plan and take action to help yourself in these tough times;
- your ability to help others cope with tough times.

What you have to do

For this assignment, you are asked to describe a situation that you have managed with a workteam in the past which was highly demanding for you and for at least some members of the team. You are asked to explain this situation and comment on it, in the light of what you have read in this workbook.

Possible situations are:

- a time of very high workload;
- a time when the future was very uncertain (for individuals, or the team, or the department or even the company);
- a time of interpersonal conflict within the team;
- a major accident or other demanding incident.

If your work experience is limited, and you have not managed a suitable situation, you could instead describe and investigate a demanding situation that affected others. (However, this option may be less useful in terms of your portfolio of evidence.)

Performance checks

The first step is simply to describe the situation as fully and objectively as you can.

The second step is to look at your own role in, and experience of, the situation. Answer the following questions:

- What was especially demanding for you personally about the situation?
- How did you experience the situation as it unfolded?
- Did you notice any physical, emotional or behavioural signs of stress in yourself?
- What did you do to help yourself cope?
- Was what you did effective in helping you cope?
- What physical, emotional or behavioural signs of stress in other members of your team did you notice?
- What did you do to help the others?

The third step is to talk to at least two members of the team who were also affected. Assure them that what you tell them will only be used for this assignment and will not be revealed to anybody else in a form that could identify them. Ask them the following questions:

- What was especially demanding for them personally about the situation?
- How did they experience the situation as it unfolded?
- Did they notice any physical, emotional or behavioural signs of stress in you?
- Do they think there was anything more you could have done or done differently to help them cope better?

The fourth and final step is to consider all the answers you have got to the above questions. In the light of what you have read in this workbook, answer the following questions:

- What now would you have done differently in this situation?
- What could you do to help your team and yourself in advance of similar situations that may arise in the future?

For example:

- If you were not sufficiently aware of the stress your team was under, what could you have monitored more carefully?
- If the steps you took to help yourself cope were not very effective, what other measures could you have taken?
- If the team did not help each other enough, what could you do to develop a higher level of teamwork?
- If there were sources of help available that you did not use on that occasion, how would you use them in the future?

Performance checks

What you should write

1 Write down your findings of the past situation, making sure that nothing is attributable to the people you talked with.

2 Include in your report a list of pointers to guide you in future demanding situations.

The whole document does not have to be more than two or three pages long.

Reflect and review

1 Reflect and review

Now that you have completed your work on *Managing Tough Times*, let's review our workbook objectives.

■ To be better able to recognize what makes your job tough

We discussed three main sources of heavy demands: the work itself; the people at work and others who indirectly affect you at work; and change. Some types of work are more demanding than others, and some times are more demanding than others. Demands can be time-based, mental, emotional or physical. Demands coming from people can be especially acute and difficult to manage. Demands from major changes are largely outside the control of individuals. But you can take measures to help you cope with these changes.

The more you are aware of the different kinds of demands and can recognize when they are likely to have a heavy impact on you or your team, the better you can take counter-measures.

You may want to ask yourself the following questions regarding these points:

■ How aware am I of the different demands placed on me and my team?

_____
_____
_____

Reflect and review

- How can I recognize when the demands from the various sources need some special response?

_____
_____
_____

The second workbook objective was:

■ To be better able to understand how you and other people typically react in tough times

Reactions to tough times are usually called stress. Stress can manifest itself in different ways, and different people have different thresholds for experiencing stress. Stress is initially a positive force, energizing people to take action. But if the stress-inducing conditions persist, then stress can cause a variety of physical and psychological problems. These range from the trivial to the life-threatening.

One question to think about is:

- What could I do to improve my ability to recognize the signs of stress in myself and others?

_____
_____
_____

The third workbook objective was:

■ To be better able to take action to help yourself and others manage tough times

There are many measures that can help combat the effects of stress. Choice of the appropriate measures will depend on the individual and the circumstances. Some of these techniques work directly on the stress reaction (e.g. relaxation or release of anger). Others work indirectly, helping to build up resistance to the effects of stress (e.g. diet, exercise). More generally, it is possible to take measures to predict when tough times may arise, so that you can be prepared, both practically (e.g. by having the right skills; building contingencies into plans) and emotionally (not being taken by surprise; using friends for moral support).

Reflect and review

Two questions to consider are:

- How could I improve my skills in the various measures for countering stress that I think would be useful for me?

- What measures would be useful to members of my team, and how could I introduce them tactfully?

The fourth and final objective was:

■ To be better able to exploit the opportunities hidden in even the toughest of times

Sometimes the worst will happen: the customer takes his order elsewhere, you lose your job, and so on. But something can always be rescued from failure. Two key things to consider are what can be learned from your experience, and what new opportunities have now opened up.

Questions to ponder in connection with this objective are:

- How can I get better at not taking failure personally and looking for the positive lessons that I can learn?

- How can I get better at uncovering the new opportunities hidden in disasters?

Reflect and review

2 Action plan

Use this plan to further develop for yourself a course of action you want to take. Make a note in the left-hand column of the issues or problems you want to tackle, and then decide what you intend to do, and make a note in Column 2.

The resources you need might include time, materials, information or money. You may need to negotiate for some of them, but they could be something easily acquired, like half an hour of somebody's time, or a chapter of a book. Put whatever you need in Column 3. No plan means anything without a timescale, so put a realistic target completion date in Column 4.

Finally, describe the outcome you want to achieve as a result of this plan, whether it is for your own benefit or advancement, or a more efficient way of doing things.

Desired outcomes			
1 Issues	2 Action	3 Resources	4 Target completion
Actual outcomes			

Reflect and review

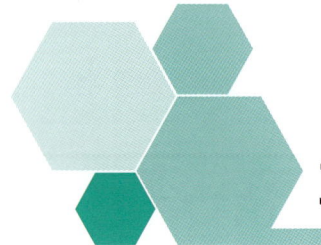

3 Extensions

Extension 1

Book   *Coping with Difficult Bosses*
Author   Robert Bramson
Edition   1993
Publisher Nicholas Brealey Publishing

This is a lively book, covering all kinds of difficult bosses, a problem not often given full attention. The strength of the book is the detailed and practical steps given for dealing with each kind of difficult boss. An important message from this book is that your own behaviour is probably an important part of any continuing problem with your manager, and that only you can take responsibility for changing your behaviour. Although you are likely to find the whole book interesting, if time is short you can quickly identify your particular type of 'difficult boss' and find a strategy for coping.

Extension 2

Book   *Stressmanship*
Author   Audrey Livingstone Booth
Edition   1985
Publisher Severn House

A comprehensive and readable account of stress. This book has three main parts: Stress and its causes; Stressmanship in action; Stress-induced illnesses and professional help. This is one of the most helpful books around on stress, giving a lot of background information on stress, as well as practical advice. There are many interesting exercises to help readers assess their own stress risks and reactions. Chapter 2 gives a detailed account of the three stages of stress, and Chapters 6 and 7 describe the different personalities and their reactions to stress.

Extension 3

Book   *Stress at Work*
Author   Joanna Gutman
Edition   1998
Publisher Sheldon Press

This workbook is designed to help you to deal with your own stress at work. It is full of case histories and exercises, which suggest different ways of reacting to pressure in your work, and to situations when other people's stress begins to affect you.

Reflect and review

Extension 4   Book   *The Manager's Guide to Counselling at Work*
                Author   Michael Reddy
                Edition   1987
                Publisher Routledge, an imprint of Taylor & Francis Books Ltd.

Although you probably do not consider yourself a counsellor, many of the skills of counselling are valuable for all supervisors and team leaders. The book is especially helpful in career direction and manpower deployment, personal problems or performance-related issues. There are three main parts: What counselling is and how it works; The skills of counselling; Counselling and the organization. Chapter 18, 'Redundancy Counselling' is especially relevant to one of the topics examined in this workbook.

Extension 5   Book   *Counselling People at Work*
                Author   Robert De Board
                Edition   1987
                Publisher Ashgate Publishing Limited

This brief, down-to-earth guide examines some of the problems people at work are likely to encounter and describes how counselling can be used to resolve them. It uses straightforward language and examples drawn from business life to show what counselling involves in practice, explains some of its underlying ideas, its advantages and also some of the pitfalls.

4 Answers to self-assessment questions

Self-assessment 1 on page 15

1 A time feels tough when the **OUTER** demands exceed your **INNER** resources.

2 When all the 'slack' has been removed from your working methods you are likely to suffer from **TIME** pressure.

3 The more tasks, people and information you have to think about, the heavier are the **MENTAL** demands of your job.

4 If you are really committed to your work, you cannot avoid some **EMOTIONAL** demands.

Reflect and review

5 Poor furniture, bad lighting, stuffy air and too much driving all add to the **PHYSICAL** demands of your work.

6 The demands you experience in your work will change according to the **PEAKS** and **TROUGHS** in your workload.

7 Examples of groups that can create demands for you in your job include:

- your line managers;
- your team;
- your customers;
- your family;
- your friends;
- yourself.

8 Examples of major changes that have tended to make working life more tough these days than in earlier times are:

- increased fear for job security;
- increases in actual redundancies;
- changing role of supervisor/team leader;
- changes in requirements for knowledge and skills;
- changing social attitudes towards authority.

Self-assessment 2 on pages 30–1

1 The three most common stressful events at work are **DISMISSAL**, **RETIREMENT** and **CHANGE IN RESPONSIBILITIES**.

2 Examples of each kind of stress symptom are:

PHYSICAL

- Headaches or migraines
- Backache
- Muscle cramps
- Poor sleep
- Indigestion
- Loss of sexual desire
- Persistent tiredness
- Skin problems
- Eye problems (e.g. double vision or difficulty focusing)
- Tingling sensations in arms or legs

EMOTIONAL

- Wild swings in mood
- Excessive worries about things that do not really matter
- Over-concern about your health
- Withdrawal and daydreams
- Inability to feel sympathy for others
- Tiredness and lack of concentration
- Increased irritability and anxiety

Reflect and review

BEHAVIOURAL

- Indecision
- Complaining unreasonably
- Becoming accident prone
- Driving carelessly
- Poor work
- Drinking more alcohol
- Smoking more
- Increased use of drugs (e.g. tranquillizers, sleeping tablets, illegal drugs)
- Eating more than usual (or sometimes eating too little)
- Change in sleep pattern, difficulty getting to sleep and waking tired

3 The two personality types most at risk from stress are the **ANXIOUS WORRIER** and the **HOT AMBITIOUS** types.

4 The name of the reaction when our bodies prepare to respond to stress is 'fight and flight'.

5 Energy in Stage II of stress is **CONSUMED**.

6 Examples of stress-related illnesses that may appear at Stage III of stress are heart disease, high blood pressure, peptic ulcers, diabetes, dermatitis, asthma, depression and gynaecological problems.

7 Causes of work-related stress include conflict with colleagues, lack of training, poor working environment, lack of equipment, lack of sufficient information to do the job, lack of appreciation, threat of redundancy, failure of management to listen, and poor corporate image.

Self-assessment 3 on pages 45–6

1 a, d, f, g and h.

2 Ways you may be able to predict tough times before they happen include your network of contacts, the economic and business news, your company's annual report and press releases, specialist magazines and journals, exhibitions and conferences.

3 If you are an anxious worrier you need to learn techniques to help you **RELAX**.

4 If you are a hot ambitious type you need to find ways to **RELEASE** your anger.

5 Keeping **FIT** is important in protecting yourself against stress.

Reflect and review

6 A **NETWORK** made up of colleagues, friends and family can be an important source of support in tough times.

7 To keep your skills future-proofed you need **TRAINING**.

8 There is always an opportunity to learn, even from the worst of **FAILURES**.

9 A **MENTOR** is someone who can help you learn from your experiences.

10 Belief in your work is strongest when your job is consistent with your **VALUES** and **AMBITIONS**.

Self-assessment 4 on page 58

1 Helping each other in tough times requires **TEAMWORK**.

2 Hope for the **BEST** but plan for the **WORST**.

3 The main emotion of someone who has been made redundant is likely to be **ANGER**.

4 Two common feelings of survivors of redundancy are **GUILT** and **FEAR**.

5 A person's **PERSONAL** problems can sometimes affect their performance at work.

6 With many problems a person just needs somebody else to help them **DEFINE** the real nature of the problem.

7 b, d, f and i.

5 Answers to the quick quiz

Answer 1 When feelings of stress, fear and threat persist you are likely to experience tough times.

Answer 2 The four kinds of work-related demands that we discussed in the workbook are time pressure, mental demands, emotional demands and physical demands.

Reflect and review

Answer 3 The groups of people whose demands often contribute to pressure at work are your team, your manager, your customers, family and friends, and yourself.

Answer 4 The jobs of many supervisors and team leaders have changed through additional responsibilities and often increased role ambiguity. These changes might add to their feelings of being under pressure.

Answer 5 Rapidly changing technology can contribute to a person's experience of a tough time through the speed at which old knowledge and skills become obsolete.

Answer 6 The most stressful event connected with working life is dismissal.

Answer 7 Examples of physical complaints that can be caused by stress include: headaches/migraines; backache; muscle cramps; poor sleep; indigestion; loss of sexual desire; persistent tiredness; skin problems; eyesight problems; tingling sensations in arms or legs.

Answer 8 As well as physical symptoms, other kinds of stress symptoms you should look out for are emotional and behavioural symptoms.

Answer 9 The types of people who are most at risk from stress are the anxious worriers and the hot ambitious types.

Answer 10 In terms of what happens to a person's energy, the three phases of stress are mobilizing energy, consuming energy, and draining energy stores.

Answer 11 Examples of measures you can take to reduce the effects of stress include: techniques for relaxation, techniques for minimizing worry, techniques for releasing anger; techniques for time management and delegation; use of support network; looking after exercise and diet; care with smoking, alcohol and drugs; taking a break.

Answer 12 Being aware early of likely threats or difficulties helps cope with tough times sometimes through making it possible to take action to fend off the tough times and always through being emotionally prepared.

Answer 13 You gain something of value from even the worst of failures through actively learning lessons from the experience and seeking to find the new opportunities that have opened up.

Answer 14 Teamwork can help people cope with tough times through members providing each other with practical and moral support.

Answer 15 Concerns of people who have not been made redundant when others around them have, include: guilt; jealousy; fear; outrage; mistrust; inadequacy; worries about the new culture.

Reflect and review

Answer 16　Counselling is a confidential one-to-one activity in which one person helps another to explore their feelings, reach a better understanding of themselves and make appropriate decisions. Mentoring is a process in which a person who has spent many years in an industry passes on his or her expertise to a younger colleague.

6 Feedback on Activity 13

The most stressful of the events in this list is death of a spouse. It is very common if one partner in a long relationship dies for the other partner to die soon afterwards. The other events can be assessed for how stressful they are by comparing them with this most stressful of events. If death of a spouse is given a rating of 100, then the full list is as follows:

- Death of a spouse   100
- Divorce   73
- Marriage   50
- Dismissal from work   47
- Retirement   45
- Sex difficulties   39
- Change in responsibilities at work   29
- Trouble with boss   24
- Change in work hours or conditions   20
- Minor violations of the law   11

7 Certificate

Completion of this certificate by an authorized person shows that you have worked through all the parts of this workbook and satisfactorily completed the assessments. The certificate provides a record of what you have done that may be used for exemptions or as evidence of prior learning against other nationally certificated qualifications.

Pergamon Flexible Learning and ILM Management are always keen to refine and improve their products. One of the key sources of information to help this process are people who have just used the product. If you have any information or views, good or bad, please pass these on.

INSTITUTE OF LEADERSHIP & MANAGEMENT
SUPERSERIES

Managing Tough Times

....

has satisfactorily completed this workbook

Name of signatory ....

Position ....

Signature ....

Date ....

Official stamp

Fourth Edition

INSTITUTE OF LEADERSHIP & MANAGEMENT
SUPER SERIES
FOURTH EDITION

Achieving Quality	0 7506 5874 6
Appraising Performance	0 7506 5838 X
Becoming More Effective	0 7506 5887 8
Budgeting for Better Performance	0 7506 5880 0
Caring for the Customer	0 7506 5840 1
Collecting Information	0 7506 5888 6
Commitment to Equality	0 7506 5893 2
Controlling Costs	0 7506 5842 8
Controlling Physical Resources	0 7506 5886 X
Delegating Effectively	0 7506 5816 9
Delivering Training	0 7506 5870 3
Effective Meetings at Work	0 7506 5882 7
Improving Efficiency	0 7506 5871 1
Information in Management	0 7506 5890 8
Leading Your Team	0 7506 5839 8
Making a Financial Case	0 7506 5892 4
Making Communication Work	0 7506 5875 4
Managing Change	0 7506 5879 7
Managing Lawfully – Health, Safety and Environment	0 7506 5841 X
Managing Lawfully – People and Employment	0 7506 5853 3
Managing Relationships at Work	0 7506 5891 6
Managing Time	0 7506 5877 0
Managing Tough Times	0 7506 5817 7
Marketing and Selling	0 7506 5837 1
Motivating People	0 7506 5836 3
Networking and Sharing Information	0 7506 5885 1
Organizational Culture and Context	0 7506 5884 3
Organizational Environment	0 7506 5889 4
Planning and Controlling Work	0 7506 5813 4
Planning Training and Development	0 7506 5860 6
Preventing Accidents	0 7506 5835 5
Project and Report Writing	0 7506 5876 2
Securing the Right People	0 7506 5822 3
Solving Problems	0 7506 5818 5
Storing and Retrieving Information	0 7506 5894 0
Understanding Change	0 7506 5878 9
Understanding Finance	0 7506 5815 0
Understanding Quality	0 7506 5881 9
Working In Teams	0 7506 5814 2
Writing Effectively	0 7506 5883 5

To order – phone us direct for prices and availability details
(please quote ISBNs when ordering) on 01865 888190